INCLINED PLANES
IN MY MAKERSPACE

by Tim Miller and
Rebecca Sjonger

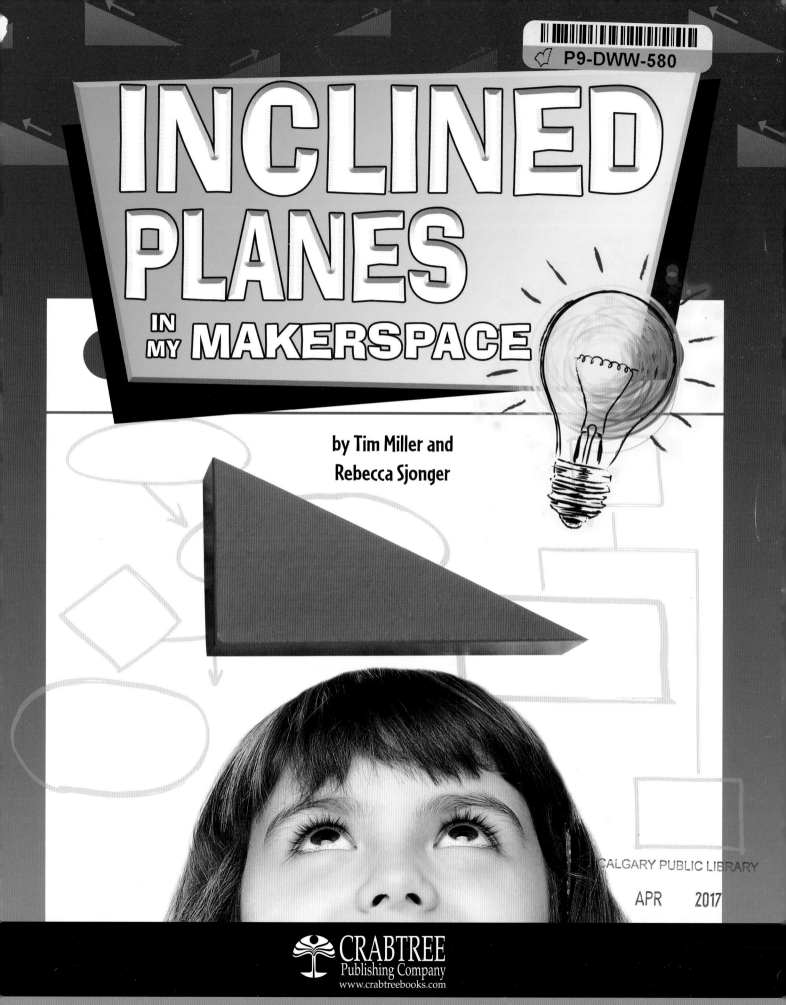

CRABTREE
Publishing Company
www.crabtreebooks.com

For Bruce and Gael

Authors: Tim Miller, Rebecca Sjonger

Series research and development:
Reagan Miller

Editorial director: Kathy Middleton

Editor: Janine Deschenes

Design: Margaret Amy Salter

Proofreader: Petrice Custance

Photo research: Margaret Amy Salter

Production coordinator and prepress technician:
Margaret Amy Salter

Print coordinator: Margaret Amy Salter

Photographs:
Shutterstock: © UKRID p16; © HuanPhoto p25
Craig Culliford: pp8-9
All other images by Shutterstock

Library and Archives Canada Cataloguing in Publication

Miller, Tim, 1973-, author
        Inclined planes in my makerspace / Tim Miller, Rebecca Sjonger.

(Simple machines in my makerspace)
Includes index.
Issued in print and electronic formats.
ISBN 978-0-7787-3370-6 (hardcover).--
ISBN 978-0-7787-3376-8 (softcover).--
ISBN 978-1-4271-1900-1 (HTML)

        1. Inclined planes--Juvenile literature. 2. Makerspaces--Juvenile
literature. I. Sjonger, Rebecca, author II. Title.

TJ147.M56 2017   j621.8   C2016-907406-4
                                        C2016-907407-2

Library of Congress Cataloging-in-Publication Data

Names: Miller, Tim, 1973- author. | Sjonger, Rebecca, author.
Title: Inclined planes in my makerspace / Tim Miller and Rebecca Sjonger.
Description: New York, New York : Crabtree Publishing, [2017] |
    Series: Simple machines in my makerspace | Audience: Ages 8-11. |
    Audience: Grades 4 to 6. | Includes index.
Identifiers: LCCN 2016054074 (print) | LCCN 2016056157 (ebook) |
    ISBN 9780778733706 (reinforced library binding : alk. paper) |
    ISBN 9780778733768 (pbk. : alk. paper) |
    ISBN 9781427119001 (Electronic HTML)
Subjects: LCSH: Inclined planes--Juvenile literature. | Simple machines--
    Juvenile literature. | Makerspaces--Juvenile literature.
Classification: LCC TJ147 .M5375 2017 (print) | LCC TJ147 (ebook) |
    DDC 621.8/11--dc23
LC record available at https://lccn.loc.gov/2016054074

Crabtree Publishing Company

www.crabtreebooks.com   1-800-387-7650

Printed in Canada/032017/BF20170111

Published in Canada
Crabtree Publishing
616 Welland Ave.
St. Catharines, Ontario
L2M 5V6

Published in the United States
Crabtree Publishing
PMB 59051
350 Fifth Avenue, 59th Floor
New York, New York 10118

Published in the United Kingdom
Crabtree Publishing
Maritime House
Basin Road North, Hove
BN41 1WR

Published in Australia
Crabtree Publishing
3 Charles Street
Coburg North
VIC 3058

CONTENTS

Do you dream up new ways to do tasks or solve problems? Do you like hands-on learning and doing experiments? Do you find creative ways to reuse everyday items? If so, this book is for you! From water slides to marble runs, the following projects will inspire you to be a maker. A maker is someone who learns by experimenting and trying new ideas. They follow their passions and create new and exciting things.

TEAMWORK

Makers often team up to share their skills and supplies. Working in a group also leads to more ideas and points of view. This sparks creativity! **Makerspaces** are places where makers work together. Some communities have makerspaces in places such as schools or local libraries. You could also set up your own makerspace and invite some friends to join you!

A new way of learning

There is no right or wrong way to make something. Makers know that:

✓ The only limit is your imagination.

✓ Every idea or question—even ones that seem silly—could lead to something amazing.

✓ Each team member adds value to a project.

✓ Things do not always go as planned. This is part of being a maker! Challenges help us think creatively.

WHAT IS AN INCLINED PLANE?

What do funnels, stairs, and skateboard ramps have in common? They all use inclined planes! An inclined plane is a sloping surface with one raised end. Some inclined planes have steep sloped surfaces. Others have less steep, or more gentle, sloped surfaces. The maker projects in this book use inclined planes.

SIMPLE MACHINES

Simple machines are tools with few or no moving parts. An inclined plane is a simple machine with no moving parts. We use inclined planes to change the amount or direction of a force. Force is the effort needed to push or pull on an object. The effort needed to use an inclined plane depends on how steep its sloped surface is. The steeper the sloped surface, the more effort is needed to use an inclined plane.

HELP WITH WORK

Inclined planes can make work easier, faster, or safer. Work is the use of force to move an object from one place to another. If you have ever played on a slide, you have used an inclined plane! Slides do the work of moving riders down to the ground quickly, safely, and easily.

INCLINED PLANES IN ACTION

Using an inclined plane means that it will take less force to move loads from one height to another. It spreads the force of lifting or lowering a load over a longer distance. A common example is someone using a ramp when loading or unloading a truck.

A ramp is a kind of inclined plane. It is safer and easier to slide or roll a heavy object up a ramp than to lift it up into the truck.

A ramp is a type of inclined plane. Building a ramp will help you understand the parts and function of an inclined plane better. You will learn that the amount of force and distance it takes to move a load up a ramp depends on how steep the ramp is. This will help you with the maker missions in this book.

Materials:

- Ruler

- Yard stick or meter stick

- Stack of books (15-20 depending on size. The stack should be at least 18 inches [45.7 cm] tall)

- Beanbag, coin, or other object that can be used as a load to test your ramp

SET IT UP!

1. Stack your books in a pile.

2. Create a ramp by resting one end of the ruler on the top of the book stack and the other end on the table.

3. Place your load at the bottom of the ramp. Using one hand, tap the object to move it up the ramp. Try your best to keep the force of each tap the same. Track how many taps it takes to move your load to the top of the ramp. Pay attention to the distance the load moves with each tap.

4. Follow steps one and two using the yard stick or meter stick.

5. Using the same load, repeat step three on this ramp. Remember to track the number of taps it takes to move the object from the bottom to the top of the ramp.

The more gentle the sloped surface of an inclined plane, the easier it is to slide a load up.

Think About It

How do the results of your ramp tests compare? Which ramp required fewer taps to move the load from the bottom to the top?

Now, think about the distance the load moved each time you tapped it. On which ramp was this distance greater?

Once you understand how a simple machine works, you will be able to modify, or change, it to solve different problems. How you build each inclined plane will change based on the criteria of each maker mission. For example, the materials, size, or type of load may change from challenge to challenge. Check out the "Modify Your Machine" boxes throughout the book.

Are you ready to get creative with inclined planes? Kick off each of the maker projects in this book by brainstorming. Try giving yourself five minutes to come up with as many ideas as possible. Write them on chart paper or sticky notes. If you work with a group, respect other people's ideas.

Once you have an idea, make a plan. Draw sketches of each part of your project. Measure everything carefully. Planning is important, but so is being open-minded. Where your project starts may not be where it ends up! Be open to changes and new directions.

Helpful hints

Running into problems is part of the maker process. If you are stuck, try some of the following tips:

- It is important to clearly understand the problem or challenge you wish to solve. Try restating the problem or challenge in your own words.

- If you are working in a group, make sure everyone understands the problem or challenge in the same way.

- Break up the problem or challenge into small parts and focus on solving one part at a time.

- **Ask:** What would happen if I changed the shape, size, or strength of a material?

- State how you will know if you have solved the problem or challenge. Fill in the blank: I will know I have solved the problem when _____.

Simple machines are some of the most basic tools—but they can improve our lives! Think about what it is like to get around in a wheelchair. How would you move from one height to another height? Wheelchair ramps are strong, sturdy inclined planes. They help wheelchairs roll over curbs or stairs.

RAMPS TO THE RESCUE

Without inclined planes, traveling in a wheelchair can be difficult. Rolling between two different heights can also be unsafe. In some cases, other people need to help lift a wheelchair over an **obstacle**, such as stairs. This takes a lot of effort to move a short distance. Using a ramp is much easier and safer.

HOW DOES IT WORK?

Inclined planes allow people to use less effort over a longer distance. For example, the force used to move a wheelchair can be spread over the length of a ramp. Imagine you must lift a wheelchair from one height to another height. It takes a lot of effort to lift a heavy object like a wheelchair straight up. Compare that with rolling the wheelchair up a ramp. When the wheelchair rolls up the ramp, you can slowly push it to the higher height instead of lifting it up.

TRY IT!

Find out for yourself how ramps make work easier and safer. Remember that makers start by planning their projects. This includes brainstorming and drawing your ideas. Flip the page to get started on the Make It Lift challenge.

Get ready to make! Build a ramp that helps move a load from a lower height up to another height easily and safely. You can choose any two heights around you—but the difference between them must be at least 6 inches (15 cm). For example, if you choose to use a desk and a chair, the height of the desk must be at least 6 inches (15 cm) higher than the height of the chair.

Materials

- Paper
- Pencil
- Measuring tape or ruler
- Ramp
- Wheeled load, such as a school bag on a skateboard

MODIFY YOUR MACHINE

Measure each height and use subtraction to make sure the difference is at least 6 inches (15 cm). You may also need to use a bigger or wider ramp to hold your load.

THINK ABOUT IT

Materials

?

Design

?

Look for varying heights you could use in your home or outdoors. What might work well for this challenge?

Size

?

What could happen if the top and bottom of your ramp are not level with the two heights?

Where will the effort come from when you move the load?

Which factors will affect how easily or safely you can use your ramp?

?

MISSION ACCOMPLISHED

Test your ramp and note the results. Did you move a load as described in the Maker Mission? If not, what could you try next?

If your ramp was a success, find ideas to mix it up on page 30.

DOWN TO THE GROUND

Some inclined planes move loads from a tall height down to the ground. They make the work of moving things easier, safer, and faster. Have you ever seen or slid down a water slide? On these inclined planes, water flows down the slide along with the riders. They carry the water—and people—from great heights quickly and safely down to the ground.

HOW DOES IT WORK?

Dropping a load to the ground is fast and easy—but not safe! An inclined plane spreads out the downward force on the load over a long distance. This means that the inclined plane slows a downward-moving load, making a safer trip to the ground. It is also fun! With a water slide, the load of water and a rider travel down the sloped surface at the same time.

ADDING PARTS

Many water slides have one or more curves to make the ride more enjoyable. Makers may also add banks, or sides, to water slides for safety. Sides that tilt inward help keep the load, or rider, from slipping off an inclined plane.

TRY IT!

Do you want to make your own mini water slide? Get started with the challenge on the next page. Use your imagination to make a splash with inclined planes and water!

The ladder or steps that people climb to get onto a water slide are also inclined planes.

Make a slide that can carry 1 cup (237 ml) of water from the top to the bottom. The height of the ramp must be at least 1 foot (30.5 cm) high. Measure the height of your ramp from the bottom to the top of the raised end. You will pour the cup of water down your inclined plane to make a mini water slide. But be careful...water cannot spill over the sides or splash out at the bottom! Collect the water at the bottom. Did you finish with the same amount of water that you started with?

Materials

- Paper
- Pencil
- Measuring tape or ruler
- Inclined plane with added sides, such as a pool noodle cut in half. Always ask an adult to help you use sharp tools.
- Materials for sides, such as rulers
- Plastic wrap
- 1 cup (237 ml) water
- Measuring cup to measure water at top and bottom
- 2 containers
- Tape, glue, etc.

MODIFY YOUR MACHINE

A water slide is an inclined plane with added features, such as sides. You also need to choose waterproof materials.

THINK ABOUT IT

Materials

How will you make your inclined plane waterproof?

Design

Where will you place a container to catch all the water at the bottom of the slide?

How high should the sides be to stop water from splashing out?

Size

How will the length and slope of your water slide affect how the water flows down it?

How will you attach sides to your inclined plane?

MISSION ACCOMPLISHED

Did you move the water down your slide without any spills? If not, what could you try next?

If your water slide worked as planned, flip to page 30 for ideas to make it even better.

Imagine a truck driving down a long, steep road. The driver discovers that her brakes are not working. Losing control of the truck puts everyone traveling on the road in danger. What might stop the runaway truck from crashing? Inclined planes could save the day!

RUNAWAY RAMPS

A runaway ramp could make the work of stopping that truck fast, safe, and easy. Runaway ramps are inclined planes placed on lanes that split away from traffic on some hilly roads. When trucks cannot stop, drivers pull onto the ramp that leads off the road.

HOW DOES IT WORK?

A steep road is a kind of inclined plane. Trucks speed up as they travel down the sloped road. If the brakes fail, a driver steers toward the runaway ramp, which has an upward-sloping surface. A force pulls the truck downward as it rolls up the sloping surface. This helps the truck slow down safely.

GAINING SPEED

TOO FAST!

TRY IT!

Make your own runaway ramp to see how this kind of inclined plane works. Gather some friends to work together and share your ideas! Get started with the Make It Stop project on the next page.

Runaway ramps are long enough to stop trucks before they reach the end of the ramp.

RUNAWAY TRUCK RAMP ↓

RUNAWAY RAMP

WHEW!

Stop a runaway object in its tracks! Make a runaway ramp that stops a rolling object before it reaches the end of the upward-sloped surface. The object should move quickly and in a straight line.

Materials

- Paper
- Pencil
- Measuring tape or ruler
- Inclined plane
- Test object, such as a toy car, small rubber ball, or other objects that roll

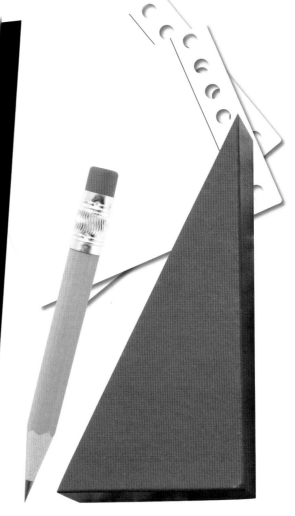

MODIFY YOUR MACHINE

Your ramp may need features to keep your test object from falling off. You will need to join the parts of your ramp together so the test object can travel smoothly down the steep road and onto the upward ramp. Use a large table space to build and test your ramp.

THINK ABOUT IT

Materials

Design

What do you need to measure carefully in this project?

What will keep the object from launching off the top of the ramp?

Try the project with different test objects. Do you need to change anything about your ramp when you switch objects? How does the challenge change?

During the planning stage, how could you test whether a steep or gentle sloped surface would work better?

MISSION ACCOMPLISHED

Find a smooth downhill path to test your runaway ramp. Launch your object to see if your ramp stops it from moving. If it does not, what could you try next?

Once you succeed at this challenge, check out the Endless Ideas on page 30.

FUN ON INCLINED PLANES

You know that inclined planes can make work easier, faster, and safer. But some of them are also fun! Can you picture the inclined planes on roller coasters? Inclined planes make up the hills on the ride. Roller-coaster cars carry people along a track that includes a series of downward and upward-sloped surfaces.

MIX IT UP

People who make roller coasters plan each part carefully. Some inclined planes make a ride move faster, just as a slide does. Others work like runaway ramps and slow down a ride. Try drawing your own ideas for using inclined planes on a roller coaster!

HOW DOES IT WORK?

Many roller coasters begin with a slow climb up a steep inclined plane. A force pulls down on the roller coaster's cars as they travel upward. At the top, the same force pulls the cars down the track on the other side, which speeds up the ride. A roller coaster gains speed from going downhill to make it up the next hill or around a loop.

TRY IT!

You might design a roller coaster someday. For now, try a simple and fun inclined plane challenge. Stick to it and you will end up with something awesome! Get started on the next page.

FAST!

SLOW

MAKER MISSION

Make a "roller coaster"—for marbles! Use three or more inclined planes in your marble run. The marble must make it through the run without falling off.

Materials

- Paper
- Pencil
- Measuring tape or ruler
- Multiple inclined planes, such as cardboard tubes
- Support materials, such as stacks of books or furniture
- Craft knife or scissors
- Tape, glue, etc.
- Marbles

MODIFY YOUR MACHINE

To make your inclined planes, choose materials with a curved surface or add sides.

THINK ABOUT IT

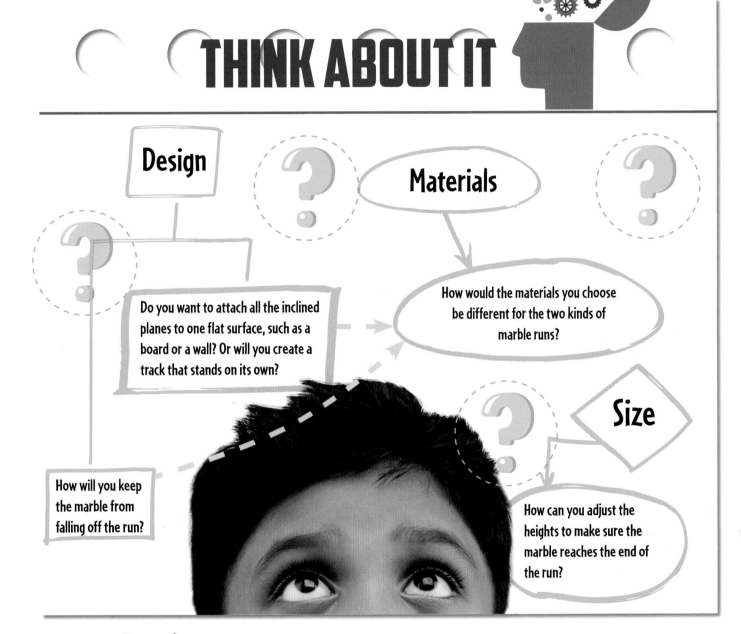

Design

Do you want to attach all the inclined planes to one flat surface, such as a board or a wall? Or will you create a track that stands on its own?

How will you keep the marble from falling off the run?

Materials

How would the materials you choose be different for the two kinds of marble runs?

Size

How can you adjust the heights to make sure the marble reaches the end of the run?

MISSION ACCOMPLISHED

Let it roll! Test your marble run and make notes about anything you need to change. Once your marble makes it through the whole run without falling off, try something new.

Find some ideas on page 30.

There are five other kinds of simple machines.
Check them out in the chart below!

NAME	PURPOSE	PICTURE	EXAMPLES
levers	move, lift, or lower objects		seesaw scissors catapult
pulleys	lift, lower, or move objects; transfer force from one object to another		flagpole zip line bicycle chain
screws	join, cut into, lift, or lower objects		jar and lid drill light bulb
wedges	split apart or lift objects; stop objects from moving		ax door stop shovel
wheels and axles	move objects		Ferris wheel rolling pin skateboard

COMPLEX MACHINES

Joining two or more simple machines creates a **complex machine**. A dump truck is an example of a complex machine. It uses an inclined plane when it raises its bed at the back to dump a load. Screws join the parts of the dump truck together. Wheels and axles allow it to move.

CHANGE IT UP!

How could you use an inclined plane and another simple machine to make a complex machine? Start by experimenting with one of the projects from this book. Flip to page 30 to get other ideas for your projects.

Makers are always learning and coming up with new ideas! You could make each of the projects in this book in many different ways. For example:

Make It Lift (pages 14–15):

- What could you do to make your design move smoothly over a flight of stairs?

Make It Slide (pages 18–19):

- How could you add curves to make the water slide more fun?
- What would need to change to add more water?

Make It Stop (pages 22–23):

- What effect would changing the ramp's surface, such as covering it with a rough material, have on how the ramp works?
- What would it take to transform your runaway ramp into a launching ramp?

Make It Roll (pages 26–27):

- How would using small balls of different sizes affect your design?
- Did you include a runaway ramp to stop the marble from rolling away at the end of the run? Try it!

LEARNING MORE

BOOKS

Christiansen, Jennifer. *Get to Know Inclined Planes.* Crabtree, 2009.

Howse, Jennifer. *Inclined Planes.* Weigl, 2014.

Law, Felicia and Gerry Bailey. *Sloping Up and Down: The Inclined Plane.* Crabtree, 2014.

Oxlade, Chris. *Simple Experiments with Inclined Planes.* Windmill Books, 2013.

WEBSITES

Get step-by-step instructions for combining inclined planes and levers to create a pinball machine at the PBS Kids website.
http://bit.ly/2fy2m8W

Check out this link to learn more about the science behind water slides.
http://science.howstuffworks.com/engineering/structural/water-slide.htm

Visit this site to learn more about inclined planes.
http://mocomi.com/inclined-plane/

GLOSSARY

brainstorming Coming up with as many ideas as possible to solve a problem or answer a question

complex machine A machine that combines at least two simple machines

effort The amount of energy, or power, used to do something

force The effort needed to push or pull on an object

inclined plane A sloping surface with one raised end

makerspace A place where makers work together and share their ideas and resources

obstacle Something that stops someone or something from moving forward; blocks the way

ramp An incline plane with a flat surface

simple machine A tool with few or no moving parts that people use to change the amount or direction of a force

steep Describes a sloped surface that has a sharp angle

work The use of force to move an object from one place to another

INDEX

ABOUT THE AUTHORS

Tim Miller is a mechanical engineer who loves to work with his hands. He is also a founding board member of Fusion Labworks, a maker community. Rebecca Sjonger is the author of over 40 children's books, including three titles in the *Be a Maker!* series.